BLUEPRINTS TO FREEDOM

An Ode to Bayard Rustin

Michael Benjamin Washington

BROADWAY PLAY PUBLISHING INC
New York
www.broadwayplaypublishing.com
info@broadwayplaypublishing.com

BLUEPRINTS TO FREEDOM
© Copyright 2023 Michael Benjamin Washington

All rights reserved. This work is fully protected under the copyright laws of the United States of America. No part of this publication may be photocopied, reproduced, stored in a retrieval system, or transmitted, in any form or by any means, electronic, mechanical, recording, or otherwise, without the prior permission of the publisher. Additional copies of this play are available from the publisher.

Written permission is required for live performance of any sort. This includes readings, cuttings, scenes, and excerpts. For amateur and stock performances, please contact Broadway Play Publishing Inc. For all other rights please contact Michael Finkle, WME, MFinkle@WMEAgency.com.

First edition: March 2023
I S B N: 978-0-88145-969-2

Book design: Marie Donovan
Page make-up: Adobe InDesign
Typeface: Palatino

CHARACTERS & SETTING

BAYARD RUSTIN, *the architect. Concert master.*
MIRIAM CALDWELL, *his assistant. 2nd violin.*
DAVIS PLATT, JR, *his former lover. Viola.*
DR MARTIN LUTHER KING, JR, *his protege. Cello.*
"MARTIN", *the human;* "KING", *the icon.*
A PHILIP RANDOLPH, *his mentor. Upright bass.*
THE ANCESTORS, *the Greek chorus. Piano.*
  Spirits made manifest through the radio; player piano and a recurring "God Light". They arrive, supernaturally, in Movement Three.

Time: Summer of 1963

Place: The March Headquarters—Harlem, New York
The Lincoln Memorial—Washington, DC
Ebenezer Baptist Church—Atlanta, Georgia

Ode: a ceremonious poem employing a triadic structure: a **strophe** followed by a metrically harmonious **antistrophe** and an **epode** (summary line) in a different metre. The three parts correspond to movements with a **chorus** in Greek drama.

This play reflects a highly educated people who read classic literature and political jargon for sport. Although the language is arched and heightened, "it's the life, not the lines".

The use of musical instruments throughout is a metaphor and not, necessarily, literal. A "Freedom Suite" is being composed following the emotional impulses and actions of the characters—a chamber orchestra in conversation.

NOTE ON MUSIC

For performance of copyrighted songs, arrangements or recordings referenced in this play, permission of the copyright owner(s) must be obtained. Other songs, arrangements or recordings may be substituted provided permission from the copyright owner(s) of such songs, arrangements or recordings is obtained, or songs, arrangements or recordings in the public domain may be substituted.

We need, in every community a group of angelic troublemakers...
Bayard Rustin, 1963

MOVEMENT ONE—
THE STROPHE; OR, TURNING BACK

Section One

(June 11, 1963)

(Lights up on a handsome parlor in an ancient brownstone turned storage space. Sections are draped in dust covers.)

(BAYARD RUSTIN, a restless lion in a cage, dials a rotary phone with one hand and opens a bottle of whiskey with the other. His suitcase and briefcase are nearby. He turns the volume down on a vintage radio crooning something like Aretha Franklin's Trouble in Mind *or Nina Simone's* Old Jim Crow.*)*

BAYARD: Harry Belafonte, please, Bayard Rustin. B-A-Y-A-R-D. R-U-S-T-I-N. Yes. No? How proficient is your short hand? Please relay I've just arrived from London this morning and realized I have yet to receive payment from our little bet last month. Prepare him for the late fee, plus penalties, plus interest, plus penalties on the interest which has turned *his* twenty dollars into *my* fifty dollars and thirty-two cents. Admonish him. Scold him. Belittle him for his delinquency and tell him, quote, I wants my monies in three-tens; two-fives; ten-ones; three nickels; one dime, and seven pennies within forty-eight hours, or else...! Read that back.

(Offstage door slams.)

MR RANDOLPH: *(OS)* Bayard!?

BAYARD: Mr Randolph!?

MR RANDOLPH: *(OS)* Bayard!

BAYARD: Phil! *(Into phone)* Have him return. *(Re: phone receiver)* Harlem, o-six-three-two. Thank you. *(He hangs up.)*

(Enter A PHILIP RANDOLPH. He carries an attache case.)

MR RANDOLPH: Bayard!! I'm tardy, forgive me—

BAYARD: Phil!! It's a quarter til six—

MR RANDOLPH: I'm tardy! I'm seventy-five—

BAYARD: Are my wires crossed? I haven't misplaced an appointment in over fifteen years. I've called everyone in my address book, twice. You said noon, no?

MR RANDOLPH: Your mind is as sharp as ever.

BAYARD: I would've called the police if I thought they'd do something. I was worried sick—

MR RANDOLPH: It got up to a hundred and two degrees today—

BAYARD: It got so hot—

MR RANDOLPH: I didn't get to open up the room this morning. I was in Washington.

BAYARD: Sweltering in here. The stale, musty scent is—

MR RANDOLPH: There is a fan to cool it off.

(MR RANDOLPH switches on the ceiling fan.)

BAYARD: Ahhh.

MR RANDOLPH: Always remember to look up, my boy!

BAYARD: *(Re: ceiling fan)* Ohh that's nice, that's lovely, Phil.

MR RANDOLPH: Can you forgive me?

BAYARD: For the very air I breathe, I do.

MR RANDOLPH: Did you sleep?

MOVEMENT ONE—STROPHE

BAYARD: You know I'm terrified of sleep. Too many wasted opportunities whilst resting. Sir, why are we here!?

MR RANDOLPH: I have an option for you. But first, let me take your temperature. How was your flight?

Bayard pours two whiskeys.

BAYARD: Deeply anxious.

MR RANDOLPH: Anxious?

BAYARD: Being summoned home from exile without an assignment has been unsettling to my spirit, sir. I'm not sure I'm ready for my next task.

MR RANDOLPH: I assume faith remains your fuel?

BAYARD: He hasn't spoken to me in a long while. Ma talks to Him for me.

MR RANDOLPH: You and God used to talk all day, everyday. What happened?

(BAYARD *offers a whiskey.* MR RANDOLPH *declines.*)

BAYARD: That still, quiet voice has been silent since… twenty-two months ago the Lord and I danced a tango that turned violent. My tongue got quicker than my filter and I said something I can't take back. He hasn't forgiven me; I haven't forgiven me. And my spirit can't cobble itself back together again 'til He speaks.

MR RANDOLPH: My my.

BAYARD: No, no I'm fine. Just fine. I assume He'll use me to the fullest, again, in due season.

MR RANDOLPH: Be still, Bayard, and say this prayer: Lord, settle my spirit and prepare my mind, for now Lord, I am ready to be used.

Bayard shoots the whiskey.

BAYARD: How are you?

MR RANDOLPH: This year I have been given the gift of reaching seventy-five years of life. For that I am grateful. However, I have stumbled upon my Great Regret. I have yet to demonstrate my life's purpose.

BAYARD: Your purpose has been on full display for decades.

(The upright bass introduces his melody.)

MR RANDOLPH: Once upon a time, unionizing the Pullman Porters was enough of a victory. Now, I want a masterpiece, Bayard. A portrait, rather. A portrait on canvas that appreciates gracefully over time.

BAYARD: Is this office your studio?

MR RANDOLPH: The church on the corner donated it to me. Us. It was used for Sunday school years ago.

BAYARD: Starting another office?

MR RANDOLPH: In part—

BAYARD: Something new?

MR RANDOLPH: —finishing something old. But wait! You always jump two steps ahead.

BAYARD: I'm impulsive.

MR RANDOLPH: You're impatient. I have just met with the Leaders.

BAYARD: And who has the Dean of Colored Leadership staffed as *Leaders*?

MR RANDOLPH: *Lord, settle my spirit and prepare my mind, for Now, Lord—*

BAYARD: What was the subject of the meeting?

MR RANDOLPH: To agree upon the 1963 March on Washington.

(BAYARD lights a cigarette.)

MOVEMENT ONE—STROPHE

MR RANDOLPH: My portrait is of an integrated America standing before the President dignified and sincere. Present our demands to the government using mass protest as a tactic within the philosophy of Non-Violence.

BAYARD: I sent you a proposal in January. You never responded.

MR RANDOLPH: I had to plant the seeds. Water them. Now, sunlight!

BAYARD: I'll be damned.

MR RANDOLPH: You'll be deputy!

BAYARD: Deputy?

(MR RANDOLPH *hands* BAYARD *a file.*)

MR RANDOLPH: I have accepted the role of Director of the March on one specific condition: I name my Deputy.

BAYARD: *(Re: file)* "The one whom will organize the greatest demonstration of racial integration for economic freedom this country has ever known."

MR RANDOLPH: Someone with the experience, passion and expertise to paint this portrait on my behalf. I hope to put forth only one name.

BAYARD: Until my past comes into question.

MR RANDOLPH: When it has come into question, I say, "I know Bayard Rustin and am pleased with the work he does for me. Maybe I should look for more homosexuals who could be so useful."

BAYARD: Are you ready this time?

MR RANDOLPH: Pardon?

BAYARD: You recited a similar passage before aborting the March of '41. Why didn't we march then? Make a grand statement?

MR RANDOLPH: The Fair Employment Act was passed. We got what we needed.

BAYARD: We got crumbs! Scraps for house dogs. No minimum wage raised. No integrated Defense til Truman. The March would've symbolized a DEMAND for a full, equal slice of equality, NOW!

MR RANDOLPH: Yes, NOW! This morning, I informed the President a march is in the planning. The turmoil in Birmingham, the lynchings. Bombings. All has escalated into a tidal wave of fear and anxiety. Now is the time for the Great March. We must stand together as one nation and insist on Our rights. We DEMAND the Civil Rights Bill be passed NOW.

BAYARD: Fusing protest with politics. Brilliant. Martin and I had great success with the Prayer Pilgrimage of '57. Almost thirty thousand people.

MR RANDOLPH: Thirty thousand? Think bigger. Grander. Half a million.

BAYARD: There's no way. A hundred thousand. Tops.

MR RANDOLPH: Don't lower the bar, my boy, raise it. Put your special touches on it. If you pull this off without a hitch, you'll have your moment. Restoration.

BAYARD: This assignment isn't for me.

MR RANDOLPH: I know you are frightened underneath that Superman facade. But don't let fear about the past win now, Bayard. We're too close. Turn back and clear my great regret, son?

BAYARD: *"I will redeem all this, on Jim Crow's head, and in the closing of some glorious day, be bold to tell you, 'I AM your son!'"*

MR RANDOLPH: Richard III—

BAYARD: No.

MR RANDOLPH: Lear?

MOVEMENT ONE—STROPHE

BAYARD: They say you used to play Billy Shakespeare to pitch perfect perfection.

MR RANDOLPH: Wait, I'm seventy-five...

BAYARD: ...Prince Hal returns home to claim his rightful place as successor to the King who also longs for...

MR RANDOLPH: ...*Peace, good pint-pot; peace, good ticklebrain—*

BAYARD: Come on, now, come on—

MR RANDOLPH: Henry IV Part One!

(BAYARD *offers the other whiskey.* MR RANDOLPH *declines.*)

MR RANDOLPH: There is a catch.

(*A grandfather clock gongs, six times.*)

MR RANDOLPH: You have two months.

BAYARD: I need four, at least.

MR RANDOLPH: And Jim Crow would happily give you a year, *but NOW is the Winter of our discontent; made glorious summer by this son of York.*

BAYARD: Mr Randolph. I'm not ready to trust this Leadership again.

MR RANDOLPH: *Lord, settle my spirit and prepare my mind—*

BAYARD: Since when did atheists start relying on prayer?

MR RANDOLPH: A lesson: it is inappropriate to force one's belief system on one's chosen staff; rather, find their source of inspiration and make that resource available. If Bayard needs reconciliation with his God, then Mr Randolph needs to supply a nice, warm thermos full of Jesus.

BAYARD: It will be an honor to paint your portrait, sir.

(The phone rings.)

MR RANDOLPH: God is ringing! And he wants to speak with you, my boy! Begin staffing immediately.

(MR RANDOLPH exits. BAYARD answers the phone.)

BAYARD: March on Washington Headquarters—Bayard speaking. Harry Belafonte! No Negro, what did your secretary tell you?! *(A beat)* On second thought, I'll see MY fifty dollars and thirty-two cents and raise you… three dozen movie stars! Well Brother Belafonte, it's THAT, or *"Day-O. Day-O. When daylight come you betta stay yo' ass home!"*

(Lights fade.)

(End of Section One)

(The radio plays a tune or the news. Perhaps, John F Kennedy, Jr's 1963 speech on Civil Rights.)

Section Two

*(Lights up. Two days later. A fresh-faced, wide-eyed woman [*MIRIAM*] sits with pad and pencil. She radiates down home charm and professional polish.)*

BAYARD: Without the use of proper nouns, tell me about yourself, Miriam.

MIRIAM: Proper nouns and proper names always clash in my mind.

BAYARD: Proper names are proper nouns. Continue.

MIRIAM: Let's see. I just graduated from…an all girls university. It's in…the South. My degree is in…this is more difficult than I thought.

BAYARD: You're doing swell!

MIRIAM: Thank you. I'm a mother. I work hard so my daughter will learn how to work hard. I was raised in extreme poverty—

BAYARD: You were *reared* in extreme poverty.

MIRIAM: I'm sorry?

BAYARD: Don't be. Continue.

MIRIAM: I want poverty eradicated. I WILL eradicate poverty. I want to be a part of History.

BAYARD: Participation in History or Make History?

MIRIAM: Sir?

BAYARD: Bayard. Do you want to be a part of a movement, participate in the events and do what you can when you can? Or, do you INSIST on change?

MIRIAM: I'm non-aggressive, politically, but not passive on my role in History.

BAYARD: I'm confused. What "role in History"? It sounds like you're ambivalent, Miriam. Not ambivalent, indifferent.

MIRIAM: No sir!

BAYARD: Bayard. Relax. It's just a test.

MIRIAM: I'm not nervous, I'm frustrated I'm not getting my point across, Sir.

BAYARD: Bayard.

MIRIAM: Mr Rustin. You of all people understand the value of human life. A life filled with hopes and possibilities. Dreams and potential. Equality, the presence of all things equal in portion and/or value… wait, focus Miriam. *(A beat)* After Dr King's arrest last month, I decided to join the youth march to free him, down home. We got as far as the park when this hateful lookin' fireman kept starin' through me. Saw his cracked lips say, "aim for her neck if you want to see it pop". Instead, he busted my ear drum open with a firehose five feet from my head. The jailhouse was full of grown folks, so they hauled us youth off to the fair grounds. Locked us in the stockyard for three days. Hungry teenagers, week old manure and the Alabama sun for three days and two nights. I've met Misery, Mr Rustin. Felt it.

BAYARD: How did you learn forgiveness?

MIRIAM: I haven't yet. *(A shift)* I engage in the same conversations concerning race as you, AND as a woman. As an educated, passionate and deeply disciplined woman who needs a mentor to teach her slash me how to... *(Re: notes)* INSIST on change. I want to work for you. I've interned for the Student Non Violent Coordinating Committee every summer for the past three summers and I can't stop. Not now, Mr Rustin.

BAYARD: Bayard. And if you play this "role in History", how, specifically, will you be the one to eradicate poverty?

MIRIAM: Honestly Bayard, I don't know.

BAYARD: You're hired.

MIRIAM: Just like that?

BAYARD: You called me, Bayard. You will be my Junior Assistant.

MIRIAM: Thank you! Please thank Mr Randolph for me?

BAYARD: You will thank him yourself. Treat him like a king, my dear. Before we begin, do you have any questions for me?

*(*MIRIAM *takes in the space.)*

MIRIAM: Is it me or does this place feel haunted?

BAYARD: The spirits of our people are in the wood.

MOVEMENT ONE—STROPHE

MIRIAM: Come again?

BAYARD: I investigated last night 'round midnight.

(BAYARD *pulls down one of many sliding panels on a built-in chalkboard. A faded notice reads:)*

MIRIAM: "Sale—Negro women and children this Saturday."

BAYARD: I believe this was an auction house then became a safe house along the Underground Railroad. Knock here.

(MIRIAM *knocks on the wall.* BAYARD *opens a hidden door.)*

BAYARD: Secret rooms. Four or five bodies could hide in there.

MIRIAM: Built to weather a storm.

BAYARD: If you're perfectly still, you can feel them.

(A pause as a strange, supernatural presence is felt by both BAYARD *and* MIRIAM. *Neither is frightened.)*

MIRIAM: Incredible.

BAYARD: Now! We have ten weeks to make this film called History you allude to starring in, so I better get you up to speed. *(He closes the hidden door, rolls up his sleeves and becomes the Great Teacher. He writes "73 DAYS TIL" on a panel on the chalkboard.)* Please begin notating the *March on Washington Pamphlet*—literature to be distributed to the masses. Remember, the average reading level is eighth grade and folks are turned off by high society or, what we call, ivy league talk. Speak plain. Also, nod to signify that you understand my instructions versus responding orally, clear?

MIRIAM: Oh, yes, Bayard. And thank—

BAYARD: Also, NOD to signify that you understand my instructions versus responding orally, clear?

*(*MIRIAM *nods.)*

BAYARD: Very good. Let's begin.

(Projections of the accented words appear, magically, on the chalkboard. BAYARD's *inner mind/*MIRIAM's *short-hand is reflected as a Ted Talk 50 years ahead of its time.)*

BAYARD: The *Washington March* will be more than just a demonstration. It will be a *living petition*, in the flesh, of thousands of citizens of *both races* unified in *purpose* and *behavior*. Not splintered into groups and individual competitors. It will be *orderly*, but not *subservient*. It will be *proud*, but not *arrogant*. It must be *non-violent*, but not *timid*. We each see *truth* from different points of views which can create *conflict*, but when a whole people speaks to its government, it's important that the *dialogue and the action* reflect the worth of that people and the *responsibility* of that government. Let's quickly discuss protocol for arrests and dealing with the police.

*(*MIRIAM *nods. Door slams.)*

MR RANDOLPH: *(OS)* Bayard!

BAYARD: On second thought, do us a favor? There is a man behind the counter at the corner deli—129 and Lenox. Tell him you work for Mr Randolph. Ask for "an update", the late edition of *The Times*, and a black coffee.

(Enter MR RANDOLPH.*)*

MR RANDOLPH: Who is this?

BAYARD: A prize intern sent up from Birmingham. Miriam Caldwell; Mr Randolph. Mr Randolph; Miriam Caldwell.

MR RANDOLPH: A pleasure, my dear. Thank you in advance for your service.

MIRIAM: The pleasure is mine, sir. *(She exits, brightly.)*

BAYARD: Now sit. The pitch!

*(*MR RANDOLPH *settles in.)*

(Projections resume.)

MOVEMENT ONE—STROPHE

BAYARD: I propose that the *1963 March on Washington for Jobs and Freedom* be a two and a half day event. *Friday*—a mass descent on *Congress* and a carefully chosen court to the *White House*. The *objective*: to flood the floors of Congress with a staggered series of *labor unions* and *civil rights* delegations from all fifty states so that the wheels of Congress will be jammed for an entire day. The *White House* delegation will pitch the *President* our proposals for both *legislative* and *executive* action. *Saturday*—a mass *protest rally*. We will introduce the *Emancipation Program* and report the response of the *President* and *Congress* to the *action* of the previous day. *Sunday*—a *non-denominational, mixed-race worship service*, for those in agreement.

MR RANDOLPH: Who is the beneficiary of this march?

BAYARD: The disenfranchised and those living in poverty.

MR RANDOLPH: Where are they?

BAYARD: Somewhere being disenfranchised and living with those in…

MR RANDOLPH: Where in my portrait? Invite them. Lots of them!

BAYARD: *How* will they get there?

MR RANDOLPH: How *will* they?

BAYARD: Give me some time to brainstorm. My body clock is off.

MR RANDOLPH: You always have a quick remedy.

(BAYARD *says nothing.*)

MR RANDOLPH: You're very smart, son, but a three day event? I don't buy the pitch.

BAYARD: The government isn't going to give us federal legislation politely. If we are not the same cowards from twenty years ago we need to fuse different forms of protest with politics!

MR RANDOLPH: We need to shift *from* protest *to* politics. You feel very empty. More battle-like than divinely inspired.

BAYARD: *(Overlapping)* Let me spell it out for you. I have old maps of Washington—

MR RANDOLPH: Is this the best you can do without that God instinct?

BAYARD: Give me 'til supper and I'll show you—

MR RANDOLPH: We won't want to ruffle the already ruffled feathers of President Kennedy.

BAYARD: Once more unto the breach, Dear Phil, once more!!

MR RANDOLPH: Leadership is reluctant about this kind of attention. Shift—

BAYARD: —from protest to politics. I will troubleshoot.

(Enter MIRIAM.)

MIRIAM: Here's your coffee and *The Times*.

BAYARD: Those are for you.

MIRIAM: I don't drink coffee.

BAYARD: You do now, trust me.

MIRIAM: Oh, Leroy at the deli says everything is copacetic. What does that mean, Mr Randolph?

MR RANDOLPH: It means all is in excellent order.

MIRIAM: May I ask you both something personal?

BAYARD: Yes, I am homosexual—

MR RANDOLPH: And no, I am not.

MIRIAM: Why do you both speak so formally?

(BAYARD looks to MR RANDOLPH.)

MOVEMENT ONE—STROPHE

MR RANDOLPH: On behalf of Our ancestors we are actively pursuing revisions to the Constitution; therefore, We should speak well and be well read on behalf of *them*. As a thank you for their services on Earth.

BAYARD: I do it to confuse white people. *(A beat)* I speak this way aloud because I speak this way to God.

MIRIAM: I don't know how you can believe in all that. With everything horrible happening in the world, it's like, Hope has died. Breaks my heart to ask, but what kind of a world are we leaving to my daughter? And who's going to save it? Him? Or, Us?

BAYARD: Well, maybe you'll meet Him at the Sunday worship service concluding the March.

MIRIAM: Sunday? No preacher in the South is gonna give up his collection plate on a Sunday. Not for a demonstration. Not with times being what they are! But what do I know, I've never even looked for God.

MR RANDOLPH: The Leaders, and I, are in agreement with Miss Caldwell. We want a Wednesday.

BAYARD: A Wednesday?

MR RANDOLPH: The ministers have congregations and need to be in the sanctuaries on Sunday.

BAYARD: But working folks cannot take off—

MR RANDOLPH: —if they are fortunate enough to have jobs they will take off.

(BAYARD *presents a Congressional chart.*)

BAYARD: No. A one day event would be a picnic not a protest! Look! I have all reactionary Republicans in red, Dixiecrats in light blue. We send a troop of six constituents to each of the congressmen, sit in and block the path…

MR RANDOLPH: Too much.

BAYARD: Non violent civil disobedience is a perfectly plausible philosophy.

MR RANDOLPH: Miss Caldwell, would you run upstairs and locate the file marked PRESS & MEDIA?

MIRIAM: Right away. *(She exits.)*

BAYARD: Are you are getting scared again?

MR RANDOLPH: I never stopped.

BAYARD: That's why you gave me the assignment. We have to make the strongest stand possible.

MR RANDOLPH: A picnic, you said?

(BAYARD says nothing.)

MR RANDOLPH: You said this is going to be more of a picnic than a protest?

BAYARD: If we lower our heads and placate the government, then yes, we should bring lemonade and fans with Jesus on them.

MR RANDOLPH: I gave you this assignment because I want Bayard Rustin to paint a portrait and mastermind a tribute to Our ancestors, but if he's Hell-bent on seeing this as his final stand—

BAYARD: I asked you if you were ready!

MR RANDOLPH: I'm directing you! I want you to paint a picture of "a door opening". I want you to hide your understandable frustrations for two months and reveal to me, to the world, that your impulsive brilliance can patiently produce a picnic. *Peace, good pint-pot,* give me peace.

(MIRIAM reenters with a file.)

MIRIAM: Here you go, Mr Randolph.

MR RANDOLPH: Thank you.

MIRIAM: So many typewriters and telephones up there.

MOVEMENT ONE—STROPHE

MR RANDOLPH: Mr Rustin has several more positions to staff, immediately.

MIRIAM: Well I'm honored to have been chosen on the spot.

BAYARD: Miriam, from here on in, I want you to be less ingratiating. However charming I need an authoritarian.

MIRIAM: Yes sir.

BAYARD: Yes what?

MIRIAM: Yes Bayard. I will review the notes we discussed then collect your supper. Will you be sitting for supper, Mr Randolph?

BAYARD: Thank you but Mr Randolph has important tasks to accomplish and my presentation isn't going to work for his event, so, your training continues.

MR RANDOLPH: You understand my wish?

BAYARD: Yes sir excuse me. *(He spots a wood frame and a swatch of muslin cloth.)* Miriam, this is wood. It can be used for sign making, carrying the injured or fire building.

MR RANDOLPH: Bayard.

BAYARD: This is muslin. It can be used for canvas or bandaging the wounded.

MR RANDOLPH: Bayard.

BAYARD: Mr Randolph, please. I have to *teach* the basics in order to *execute* the basics. So Miriam, let's make a big ass SIGN! *(He places the muslin on the ground and throws the frame on top of it.)*

MR RANDOLPH: Pouting like Little Boy Blue.

BAYARD: Phil, I believe in non violence; I believe in you; but, believe you me, when provoked I can forget myself. Let me toss a little wood.

MR RANDOLPH: In order to wrangle this delegation of Leaders you will need a few laps around the mountain of Patience. Learn when to "demand now" and how to gracefully wait.

BAYARD: You should write a book, Phil, and fill it with all your wit.

MR RANDOLPH: HOLD!! This flip, smart ass mouth you found might sing in London but it don't swing in Harlem, boy! Remember yourself. Quick. I'll leave the PRESS & MEDIA file here for your review. Wednesday, August 28th. One day demonstration. Press release ten AM tomorrow. Now, you've had "some time to brainstorm". How are my disenfranchised Southern guests being transported to Washington?

(Silence.)

MIRIAM: *(Re: imaginary notes)* Mr Rust—Bayard asked me to inquire about the fleet of buses you all put out of work during the '55 bus boycott. He's "certain they'll welcome the integrated business". *(She stands tall.)*

MR RANDOLPH: Thank you, Miriam. Would you call ahead to Hotel Lorraine and confirm my reservation for two. Tell them I'm tardy. Tell them I'm seventy-five. I know Dr King's schedule is packed.

(MIRIAM nods and exits.)

BAYARD: Martin?

MR RANDOLPH: Speak plain.

BAYARD: I have to come with. He and I need to discuss what happened.

MR RANDOLPH: Whoa. Whoa. Whoa. He, too, is walking the tightrope of faith and your tone alone will push him off. We can't afford to lose him.

BAYARD: Lose him? This is not the assignment for me.

MOVEMENT ONE—STROPHE

(A beat)

MR RANDOLPH: *(Calling off)* Miriam!?

MIRIAM: *(OS)* Yes sir?

MR RANDOLPH: *(Calling off)* Inform Roy Wilkins at the NAACP there has been a major change in plans.

BAYARD: Wait.

MR RANDOLPH: No, you will wait. You will practice patience for one week, then you may speak, carefully, to Martin.

(MIRIAM re-enters.)

MIRIAM: What was that sir?

MR RANDOLPH: False alarm, dear. Thank you. *(He exits.)*

MIRIAM: What should I do?

Bayard lets off steam via a staple gun connecting wood to muslin. Projections resume.

BAYARD: *"Wait"*, he says! Wait? The *current crisis* is overwhelmingly the result of structural unemployment, and he says, *wait*! *Negro unemployment is almost three times higher than white workers*, breeding *misery* and *frustration* in every community—*North and South. Automation* is attacking the unskilled and *semi-skilled* jobs to which Negroes have traditionally been relegated, but he wants to wait! This is exactly why I once lost faith in him in back in '41.

MIRIAM: Who broke what? I know boys break things.

BAYARD: He broke a promise and I can feel him giving up again.

MIRIAM: What are the solutions for this? NOW. Our active, doable solutions.

BAYARD: The same solutions as then, this demonstration, but I feel—

MIRIAM: Be specific.

(BAYARD *lights a cigarette.*)

MIRIAM: That smoke isn't going to free our people any faster, at some point you'll have to use your words, Bayard. *(A beat)* I have a two year old. She can't talk much yet but she loves to throw her wooden blocks just like you.

BAYARD: The comparison to a toddler is secretly flattering. We'd all be so lucky to return to life before we learned what the world really is, but a female child? Are you insinuating something?

MIRIAM: In most cases, a man in this professional situation would have taken the first woman he sees and ordered her to do something, anything. A woman in the same professional situation would have three new options, two backs ups, and at least one man she'd have to give the credit to.

BAYARD: I understand, but I feel if we don't—

MIRIAM: "Feelings." Freshman year, Professor Hollis, "Never lead with your feelings. There's always 'some man' waiting 'round the corner ready to take your power if you're willing to give it." I didn't leave my baby in the heat of the South to watch a great man guess at victory. Why do we march?

(Projections resume. MIRIAM *notates.)*

BAYARD: We march to redress old grievances and help resolve...an American crisis born of the twin evils of racism and economic deprivation. They rob all people, Negro and white, of dignity, self-respect, and freedom.

MIRIAM: Very good. Organize the demands. I'm ready.

(BAYARD *stares blankly at the chalkboard.*)

MIRIAM: Bayard?

MOVEMENT ONE—STROPHE

BAYARD: I'm stuck. Planner's Block. Damn! *(Re: sign)* What do you see when you look at this canvas?

MIRIAM: A poor stapling job. You're not supposed to crawl all on top of the muslin…

BAYARD: Metaphorically.

MIRIAM: I see my cause.

BAYARD: Which is?

MIRIAM: The blank future for women in this country.

BAYARD: INSIST on change, then. Show me how you see.

(Projections resume in MIRIAM's handwriting.)

MIRIAM: Well, Mr Randolph seems to like, *DEMAND*, so…I *DEMAND* my *government* uphold my *Constitutional rights* as a *woman* with the same *verve and integrity* extended to *men*. As the *leaders* of the *March on Washington* taught me, *"don't wait a hundred years* to stand up and tell your *elected officials* what the *masses demand"*.

BAYARD: You've practiced this?

MIRIAM: In the shower.

BAYARD: Three brief examples.

(BAYARD studies this violin's clear tone and confident pitch.)

MIRIAM: One. *Safe legal abortions*. Two. *On-site day care* extended to working mothers. Three. *An Equal Employment Opportunities Program,* allowing us to *fully integrate* into a society that should be retiring *exclusionary practices*.

BAYARD: Challenge: How can you justify speaking on behalf of the Negro woman whose life in poverty and race-based discrimination doesn't align with your movement?

MIRIAM: The financial discrepancy in pay between a man and a woman far exceeds that of race. *ALL women earn* less because of gender.

BAYARD: According to whom?

MIRIAM: President Kennedy signing the *Equal Pay for Equal Work Bill* five days ago. The *Civil Rights* movement *should* be a *Human Rights* movement.

(Projections end.)

BAYARD: Impressive, Maid Miriam. Impressive.

MIRIAM: I agree. *(Re: newspaper)* I read about the bill signing while Mr Randolph was cursing you out. Your turn. Dig deep. What does your gut tell you? What are our demands?

(Silence)

BAYARD: I need to make a call.

MIRIAM: What should I do?

BAYARD: Good question. Tell me what you figured when I conclude.

MIRIAM: *(Re: PRESS & MEDIA file)* I suppose this press release and pamphlet aren't going to write themselves.

BAYARD: I like you, Miriam. I really do. You mentioned you've never looked for God. Childbirth? You didn't meet Him? That seems the perfect moment, no?

MIRIAM: I blacked out. Trust me when I tell you I wouldn't remember if God, Satan or Mr Randolph snatched that child outta me. But, I got, how would *you* say it, ummm… *"a beautiful engine named Lillian to drive with"*. Yeah yeah, there go Bayard, that sounds JUST LIKE you!

BAYARD: Would you say she watches over you?

MIRIAM: Yeah. I like that. My baby watches over me.

MOVEMENT ONE—STROPHE

BAYARD: You've been very transparent, Miriam. One truth about me: I like that you don't apologize for your statements.

MIRIAM: You are a rare man, indeed. I'll go set up reception. You get a new idea. *(She exits.)*

(BAYARD *discovers a set of pocket doors and slides them shut.)*

BAYARD: *(Addressing the heavens)* Ma! I'm sorry, I know, 'call as soon as I land', but there's been an urgency in the air all week and I've had to dash quickly. Ma, I'm out of Divine fuel and my livelihood depends on it. If you are passing by the Lord sometime this evening, ask Him to…settle my spirit and prepare my mind and favor me with discernment. Tell the Ancestors, 'thank you for holding onto me'. I can feel you, All. Even when God is silent. I LOVE YOU, MA!

MIRIAM: *(OS)* What was that??

BAYARD: Nothing, Dear. Just calling home.

(The grandfather clock gongs, six times.)

(An idea strikes BAYARD *as* Just A Closer Walk With Thee *tinkles in on the piano, playing itself, magically. The* ANCESTORS/*spirits in the wood are made manifest through the piano.)*

(A golden God light—or, God's constant presence, slowly baths BAYARD *and the piano, unbeknownst.)*

(Bayard sees a vision appearing on the chalkboard panels:)

(Projection of Dr Martin Luther King's out-stretched hand waving over a sea of people.)

*(*BAYARD*'s temperature rises as he begins transforming the room from a eerie storage space into a cozy office.)*

(End of Section Two)

END OF MOVEMENT ONE

MOVEMENT TWO—
THE ANTISTROPHE;
OR, TURNING AGAINST

Section One

(Lights up. Six days later. 8 AM. BAYARD *listens to music on the radio.)*

(He writes "67 Days Til" on the board.)

(A knock on the door.)

BAYARD: Slide it.

(Enter MIRIAM. *She turns off the radio.)*

MIRIAM: Bayard! Dr Martin Luther King, Jr. is here to see you. Wait! In case I never utter that introduction again. BAYARD! THE DR MARTIN LUTHER KING, JR is here to see you!!

BAYARD: Thank you, Miriam.

(Enter MARTIN.*)*

MARTIN: Yes, thank you, Miriam. Very nice introduction.

MIRIAM: Thank you! I practiced! My girlfriends and I ditched graduation to bust you out of jail, but it didn't work!!

MARTIN: Oh. And where was school?

MIRIAM: Spelman.

MARTIN: Morehouse.

MIRIAM: I KNOW! *(She squeals.)*

MIRIAM: Coffee? Tea? THE Reverend Dr Martin Luther King, Jr?

MARTIN: Coffee. Black, please. I could use a pick me up this morning. And thank you, Miriam, for the coffee AND the cavalry.

(MIRIAM nods and exits.)

MARTIN: Bayard.

BAYARD: Martin.

(Strict tension sings.)

MARTIN: How have you been?

BAYARD: I'm well, minister.

MARTIN: I'm returning your copy of The Gandhi Reader. Thank You.

(MARTIN hands BAYARD the book. BAYARD tosses it.)

MARTIN: Well. Mr Randolph asked me to drop by and check in. So. *(He begins to exit.)*

BAYARD: The reservations at Hotel Lorraine were to your liking?

MARTIN: I don't eat like that even at Thanksgiving. Humongous Porterhouses! And we drank. My God, my God, we drank.

(BAYARD aggressively shifts panels on the chalkboard.)

MARTIN: You look like you slept here.

BAYARD: I don't sleep, but I did spend the evening here after taking in a late film.

MARTIN: Which one?

BAYARD: *Cleopatra*. Have you seen it?

MOVEMENT TWO—ANTISTROPHE

MARTIN: Well, you'd be proud of me. I was jailed for practicing the non violent techniques you taught me. So, no, I haven't found a moment to see any films.

BAYARD: Well, I have lots of free time. As a burdensome and expendable "sexual pervert", I—

MARTIN: Never expendable, Bayard.

BAYARD: And never spared. Last night after I finished my calendar I went to witness the million-dollar paycheck Ms Elizabeth Taylor has tucked in her pocketbook. The chronicles of the young Queen of Egypt as she resists the imperialist ambitions of Rome. Whilst banished from our movement here at home I went to Rome. Then to Egypt, which is in Africa. Then to protest nuclear testing in the Sahara Desert, also in Africa. You know what amazes me, Minister?

MARTIN: No, what?

BAYARD: It amazes me that in Africa—with *Our* people—same hue, same hair, same noses and the like, *Our* people—seem to concern themselves with only one characteristic concerning me. My ability. My ability to speak the truth and speak it to the highest power. Speak Truth to Power, we'd chant. My ability to organize. To live my birthright as a Quaker. To live and teach the true meaning of Jesus Christ, not just preach it from a pulpit—

MARTIN: Bayard, I—

BAYARD: Please minister, I've waited to breathe, let me. When I was passed over as head of the Southern Christian Leadership Conference, which I set up so you could speak as the head and not the tail, I played it humbly. Wasn't my time. When it was time to excuse myself from the movement because of the threat I'd be exposed, I did so, gracefully. Eventually I fell back into the good graces, or at least the tolerance, of Leadership.

But when you dismissed me from the movement because of a *lie*...

(MARTIN *stiffens.*)

BAYARD: An intentional falsehood concocted by a rival Negro leader. A Congressman. A minister, who functioned under the direct command of the leaders of the House and the Senate, you never thought for a second to spare me. You let Adam Clayton Powell remove me from the movement because of A LIE.

MARTIN: When Adam threatened to expose you and me as homosexual lovers I had one choice. He did concoct a lie. I did turn against you. We have been derailed. But that was two years ago and God has brought you and me back together—

BAYARD: —Ooooh shiiiit—

MARTIN: —not to agree on the past or even understand it, but to be mature and God fearing enough to overcome our differences.

(Re-enter MIRIAM. *She sets down the coffee and exits.*)

BAYARD: I understand you have reservations about the March?

MARTIN: The SCLC is participating in the March.

BAYARD: And you?

MARTIN: Something happened inside that jail cell in Birmingham, Bayard. I sat in there scribbling notes on toilet paper. Scribbling on the edges of newspapers trying to get it out of me articulately. I prayed, Lord use this for your Glory, and He said, *"receive this Word"*, so I meditated on it. I prayed, Lord, stop this burning sting of hatred. He said, *"I have sent you the healing balm"*, and daily I look for it. But then I heard ol' Bull Connor whip out fire hoses and unleash bloodhounds on our babies. Washin' 'em down the

MOVEMENT TWO—ANTISTROPHE

street like diseased trash and still no word from the Kennedy Boys. Still don't believe this is a real moral issue. I prayed, Lord, tell me why the children have to get hurt so bad? How can you let them hurt our babies so? I challenged my God, Lord, give me the understanding to sooth my blistered people. Now, Lord! And He was silent for hours. Starin' at the ceilin' in the dead of night exhausted and too angry to drop a tear, I gave over. And then, He came. A warm, white light. A brilliant white light stood tall in my cell. He spoke. *"Be still and know that I am God"*. I shut my mouth, rolled over on my cot and let myself shed a tear. For those children outside. And for the unsettled feeling that it's not over. Hate breeds itself down there. It's not over. God spoke it to me. I heard Him. But something has shifted in me, shifting in me the wrong way. As I look for the healing balm; look for the shade tree to point our weary, blistered people to, why do I keep stumbling over our people who shout 'sellout and Uncle Tom' for doing God's Will? My own people won't let me into their churches because *my message* is too controversial? Why would the church, my people shut me out?

BAYARD: Fear. Fear that if you succeed and show that unity is possible then a new normal must begin. Fear has been programmed into us.

MARTIN: But shut out AND alone?! I wasn't prepared for my own people to shut me out! Out here with this weight on my shoulders!

(The irony is lost on MARTIN.*)*

MARTIN: Why won't He send me the healing balm to soothe our people?

BAYARD: You know what the healing balm is, Brother Moses.

MARTIN: I don't like wearing the cloak of Moses.

BAYARD: And yet his rod and staff fit you perfectly. You are one of the greatest interpreters of the Old Testament in this country. All those sermons on the Book of Exodus and you're telling me you've never rehearsed the role of Moses?

MARTIN: The responsibility of being Martin has kept me busy.

BAYARD: Let me see your education, Reverend King. Exodus 33:1—

MARTIN: *(Instantly) Then the Lord said to Moses, You and the people you brought out of Egypt must leave this place. Go to the land I promised to Abraham, Issac, and Jacob.*

BAYARD: 33:12.

MARTIN: *Moses said to the Lord, You have been telling me to lead these people, but you have not let me know whom you are sending with me.*

BAYARD: You're focused on who's going to share the spotlight and the burden, but this is a singular assignment. I know you were scared Brother Abernathy wasn't with you in that cell. First arrest ever without him. But that warm, white light came because you were alone. You're focused on 'whom you're sending with me'. 33:12-13.

MARTIN: *Moses said to the Lord, You have been telling me to lead these people, but you have not let me know whom you are sending with me. You have also said, I know you by name, and I am pleased with you.*

BAYARD: *I know you by name, and I am pleased with you. I will do what you have asked, because I am pleased with you, and I know you by name.* He took you to that rocky cleft and covered you, Martin. He delivered through you a stone tablet document in the form of *Letter from Birmingham Jail*, didn't He? Bathed you in warm, bright white light, didn't He? *(His jealousy rises.) The Lord came*

MOVEMENT TWO—ANTISTROPHE

down in a cloud and stood there with you and called out his name "The Lord"—

MARTIN: —*"The Lord", always faithful and ready to forgive.*

BAYARD: The Word is the balm, Martin.

MARTIN: Bayard. I am sorry about the hurt these past events have caused you and I sincerely pray for your forgiveness.

BAYARD: Can Mr Randolph confirm your presence at the March? We need a keynote address.

(A beat)

MARTIN: Yes. Yes he can. The tone?

BAYARD: Those children that you mentioned being "washed down the street". If Moses suggested forty years equals a biblical generation, what do you want for them at the turn of the century?

MARTIN: I've had a dream. I. I dreamed...I won't live to see forty years. I. I also stopped by to see if you had any counsel on this. If I accept the cloak of Moses, why would God have us lead, sacrifice, wander and die without ever entering the Promised Land? *(He lights a cigarette.)*

BAYARD: You and Moses were reared in extreme privilege. Pharaoh's palace. Access. Opportunities. Lifestyle. You thrive amongst Negro and White brilliance. Benefit from the privileges of integrated life and know what you're fighting for. Moses led the Israelites to milk and honey because he was reared knowing what it looked like, tasted like. Consider: God doesn't let you two enter the Promised Land because He already let you both live there.

MARTIN: I've always been drawn to you because you too were reared to hear His calls. Why didn't He come to you?

BAYARD: He did. Eighth grade. You know how hormones scare you when they first arrive? One afternoon at school the feelings got so strong I ran to the boys room and sang and prayed and cried. I told God to "fix these thoughts or I'm done! I'M DONE!" I can be very dramatic, I know, but I threw my hands up, fell to my knees, and out of nowhere the most beautiful, vivid, cooling white light poured into the boys room. He spoke. "Do you trust me enough to stand in the center of exactly who I made you to be? Yes or no?"

MARTIN: You said...?

BAYARD: I wanted to say, Yes, I trust you. I was mesmerized by the gentleness of His grace. I was so young, I was stunned into silence. I didn't say, Yes. Then, years later, He called. About you. I accepted the role of Aaron to your Moses. *And Moses went up on the mountain of God. He told the Leaders, "Wait here. Aaron is with you. Take all your disagreements to him".* But since you and I fell out twemty-two months ago, I've been waiting and wandering and waiting for that sweet light to shine on me, again. To hear His voice, again. To say, Yes, I trust you, again. *(A shift)* Minister. I need you. My pride hates saying that, having to ask for that or for anything, but I do. If History repeats himself, I need you to convince the leaders that you vouch for me. I need you to stand up for me and say, "I know Bayard Rustin, and am pleased with him". Help me erase this blemish.

MARTIN: We can't control God's will nor estimate His timing. But if we remain disciplined and obedient, then all good things will be added unto you.

MOVEMENT TWO—ANTISTROPHE 33

(BAYARD *stiffens.*)

MARTIN: You sure you're ready to be the Deputy of these bad boys? Mr Randolph, myself and James Farmer are all of one accord, but not Roy Wilkins. John Lewis is a lit fuse and Whitney Young won't commit. Plus, my God, my God, if there was a totem pole, ALL of us'd be tryin' to stand at the top on tippy-toe.

BAYARD: What's Roy Wilkins's concern?

MARTIN: Your sexuality has been an ongoing concern. Many view it as the Scarlet Letter.

BAYARD: Oh. I thought the Scarlet "A" was for Adultery, minister.

(MARTIN *extinguishes his smoke.*)

MARTIN: Again. I am sorry for the hurt these past events—

BAYARD: —but that doesn't help me understand it.

MARTIN: Your time in the Young Communist League *also* complicates things. The FBI is forcing me, threatening me to remove ALL Communist influences from this movement or be exposed for my trespasses and here you come hollerin' "I want to be used exactly as I am". Play-actin' a Peacemaker after stirrin' up most of the mess in the first place! Talkin' 'bout, "I accepted the role of Aaron". Please! You are instinctive. Aggressive. Too confident about your own abilities. You're just like Joshua. Boxing God. Taking down armies on impulse. But Joshua didn't win the battle of Jericho because of his sword, Bayard, he won because of his worship. And you still refuse to stand in the center of your light, according to *His* will. But it's lucky for you Mr Randolph knows Joshua WILL win the battle. And because I trust you, and if I have your forgiveness, I will do what you have asked because I am pleased with you and I know you by name.

(BAYARD *hands* MARTIN *The Gandhi Reader.*)

BAYARD: And they say our shining new star is burning out of gas.

(Intercom buzzes.)

MIRIAM: *(OS)* President Kennedy's office. It's urgent.

BAYARD: *(Into intercom)* Tell him I'm concluding counsel with King.

MARTIN: God invites us to challenge Him, but He only comes once we surrender all to His will.

(BAYARD *answers the phone.*)

BAYARD: March Headquarters, Bayard speaking. Happy Juneteenth, Bobby. Juneteenth: the day the slaves in Texas...ask Lady Bird. Listen, we'll confirm this afternoon but I'd plan on The Big 6 including Mr Randolph AND Dr King...

(MARTIN *exits.*)

BAYARD: ...plus Dorothy Height to ensure you gentlemen stay on your *Ps and Qs*. Also, in light of the Medgar Evers assassination this week, we need two bodies approved by you and the President covering Dr King from sun up to the podium to sun down on the day. *(A beat)* Well the press on this event can go another way, sir. *(A beat)* I understand that, Mr Kennedy. WELL IF AT THE CONCLUSION OF DR KING'S ADDRESS, ONE OF YOUR BOYS DOESN'T MATRICULATE OUT OF THIN AIR AND FALL ON HIM LIKE A FRESH COAT OF LOTION, IT WILL! Because I'd like NOT to see any more of our leader's heads blown off in front of their wives and children. Federal troops? Bobby!

(Thunder. Power goes out.)

(Dimly lit, the room takes on a mysterious romanticism.)

(BAYARD *leaves the receiver off the hook on top of the piano.*)

MOVEMENT TWO—ANTISTROPHE

(End of Section One)
(Time passes.)

Section Two

(Power is [still] down. A rainy late afternoon, August 13th. Mother Nature plays an aggressive symphony outside.)

(Sweaty, Bayard sits at the piano in his soiled undershirt. He plays a bluesy spiritual as a golden God light baths him. The phone is [still] off the hook. Singing:)

BAYARD:
All night, all day
I know the angels,
Keep watch—
O'er me, my Lord.
All night, all day
I know the angels,
Keep on watchin—
O'er me, my Lord.
(He retrieves the dangling phone. Into phone) That's a favorite from the chain gang, or you could do, *He's Sweet, I Know*…just not *Amazing Grace*. Something extra special, Sister, you're opening for Martin. *(He jiggles the receiver. No luck.)* Hello. Sister Jackson?? Miriam!! I've lost Mahalia in the storm. Get her back.

MIRIAM: *(OS)* The power is down!

BAYARD: Use the intercom!

MIRIAM: *(OS)* The power is down!

(BAYARD writes "15 Days Til" on the board. MIRIAM bursts in.)

MIRIAM: You have a visitor.

BAYARD: Who is it?

(Enter DAVIS PLATT JR, *a soaking wet, preppy, white gentleman carrying a brown paper bag and suitcase. He pants for air.)*

MIRIAM: Bayard!? Mr Davis Platt. Coffee or tea, Mr Platt?

BAYARD: Hey there, pal.

*(*MIRIAM *exits.)*

DAVIS: I know, never disturb you when you're working but—

BAYARD: Never a nuisance.

DAVIS: Are you alright?

BAYARD: Are *you* alright!?

DAVIS: I'm drenched.

BAYARD: Yes you are. I saw a box of socks and T-shirts around here—

DAVIS: No! There are trains at 6:45, 7:10 and 7:25 out of Penn Station.

BAYARD: Heading where?

DAVIS: West towards California. I tried to call…haven't you heard?

BAYARD: Heard what?

(A beat)

DAVIS: If you could spare socks. I don't want to catch cold.

BAYARD: Yes. Take off those wet things and let your jacket dry.

DAVIS: Thank you.

*(*BAYARD *searches for dry garments.)*

*(*DAVIS *removes his wet jacket, shirt, socks and shoes.)*

MOVEMENT TWO—ANTISTROPHE 37

DAVIS: You've heard…they're demolishing glorious Penn Station in favor of an eye sore sporting facility? I'm taking one last classy adventure out of town before it becomes a crowded hamster cage.

BAYARD: Are you going to California with someone?

DAVIS:
O, beware, my lord of jealousy;
It is the green-ey'd monster which—

BAYARD: I am not jealous.

DAVIS: Stop. I understand you.

(BAYARD *has found a towel and begins drying* DAVIS *off.*)

DAVIS: It's my birthday.

BAYARD: Well. Happy Birthday, Pal! I forgot.

DAVIS: It's alright. You never remembered. I mean I never reminded you. It seemed silly celebrating the day I was born when you were on real missions. Serving great purpose.

BAYARD: I'm sorry if I neglected you.

DAVIS: Serving two years for religiously rejecting the draft should not be mistaken for neglect.

BAYARD: Thank you for writing me everyday.

DAVIS: *Desdemona* wrote you everyday, *Davis* was never allowed in.

BAYARD: The storm is outside but the lightning strikes in here.

(DAVIS *says nothing.*)

BAYARD: You burst in here like the Klan was chasing you. What can I do for you?

DAVIS: Let me look at you. You're drinking. From the looks of it not sleeping. Not that you ever did. Who is taking care of you?

BAYARD: Who are you meeting at Penn Station?

(A standoff)

(DAVIS, wanting the melody, walks around the office, barefoot, with the towel around his shoulders.)

DAVIS: This is huge!

BAYARD: The room?

DAVIS: The event, the press. My goodness, the press. I've kept up with your whereabouts through clippings and newspaper articles. Deputy. They've invited you back in. For the moment.

BAYARD: A moment if we're lucky, an event if we're blessed. *(Investigating the paper bag)* Is this...?

DAVIS: It's just honey-glazed turkey with tomato and romaine on a slightly toasted English muffin.

BAYARD: You make this sandwich better than Ma used to.

DAVIS: There's also beef and carrot stew, or, sweet pickles and a Coca-Cola if you want something light.

BAYARD: Made with love. You can taste it.

DAVIS: Can you? *(Silence. He removes the towel.)* The storm is getting worse and I don't want to get all dry and comfortable just to get drenched again.

BAYARD: So you came to bring me dinner?

DAVIS: I came to tell you...I came to ask you...

BAYARD: Davey?

DAVIS: I jogged thirty blocks in the rain without an umbrella because you always said "show me don't tell me". I'm showing you. I'm showing up for you. Here I am, but—

BAYARD: And you look wonderful, but, what?

MOVEMENT TWO—ANTISTROPHE

DAVIS: My timing is terrible, I know. And you need to focus. I know. And I don't want to complicate your…, but someone needed to show up for you.

BAYARD: Davis, this isn't the most appropriate—

DAVIS: Why won't you let anyone get close to you? Your brilliance. Your flaws.

BAYARD: I play my cards close to the vest.

(BAYARD *tosses* DAVIS *a dry shirt.*)

DAVIS: You're scared.

BAYARD: Do you know what would happen if somebody walked in and saw a half naked white… We were us years ago, a lot has shifted since.

DAVIS: Nothing's shifted. Men don't shift. We grow accustomed to our flaws and learn to justify them.

BAYARD: What's this preoccupation with flaws? When did this splinter get lodged into your soul?

DAVIS: Why didn't you fight for me? Wasn't I good enough to fight for?

BAYARD: Fight whom for you, Davis?

DAVIS: The ones who refuse to give you your due because you're gay!

BAYARD: Gay??

DAVIS: Homosexuals who hate "queer" are trying "gay". It's progressive.

BAYARD: It'll never play! Gay??

DAVIS: Negroes who have contempt for "Colored" are trying to get Dr King to say, "Black Power!" Keep up, old man.

BAYARD: "I'm a gay, black man." There's no music to it.

DAVIS: —don't change the subject. You always wit me out of—

BAYARD: —should I wear a nametag that says, Hi. I'm a Negro-Gay-Black-Pacifist—

DAVIS: DON'T MOCK ME. You go out and march and fight for the future of your people. Your people! Not just Negro, but gay, too. You belong to more than one community.

BAYARD: The Leaders haven't even gotten their due, yet. I'm not mocking you, Davis—

DAVIS: I'm not concerned with The Leaders. *You* are a leader. I love *YOU*. *(He puts the shirt on.)* Silence. You can speak to kings and queens about anything under the sun, but for the one man who shows up for you you're speechless? Why are you still justifying their lives over ours?

BAYARD: I have never been ashamed and I have never hidden.

DAVIS: You got arrested in the back of a parked car with two men.

(BAYARD stops cold.)

DAVIS: Never ashamed, huh? You've become comfortable standing AND playing in the shadows. Getting these "Leaders" immortalized is more important than someone who wrote you everyday in code. Are they still more important than the same someone who is trying to tell you your name is important too? Tell me was I good enough?

BAYARD: You've come closest to understanding me but I fear you don't know me at all.

DAVIS: I know if there's an integrated bus to Heaven, these Leaders would have us march behind it.

(The power turns back on. The RADIO *mumbles, softly.)*

BAYARD: The making of a movement is about marketability so I cast myself where I can work. Mr

MOVEMENT TWO—ANTISTROPHE

Randolph wants a pretty picture for his seventy-fifth birthday and he asked ME to paint it. If I succeed, maybe, maybe the Lord will finally use me, exactly as I am, to the fullest. Then, then when I'm seventy-five, then—

DAVIS: —then I hope there is someone there to paint one for you. Particularly if you don't have children of your own.

(Enter MIRIAM. *She spots a dressing* DAVIS *and exits.)*

MIRIAM *(OS. Intercom)* The phones are up and ringing off the hook. Phil said he'd be over immediately.

BAYARD: MR RANDOLPH. Thank you.

DAVIS: What time have you?

BAYARD: *(Re: pocket watch)* It's Six.

(DAVIS *abruptly turns off the radio. He puts on the dry socks and wet shoes.)*

DAVIS: I didn't come to yell at you. Although it felt good. You speak of God's will. Does that inner voice you allude to say He sent me for you? Then and now?

BAYARD: I lost it, Davis. That precious light has dimmed in my soul. My heart says yes, but…

DAVIS: Then come with me. NOW. I want you. Not out of desperation but certainty.

BAYARD: I'm not ready to be your one and only.

DAVIS: He sent you for me.

BAYARD: I'm not a perfect man. If I am to live with myself in this world any longer sex must be expressed differently.

DAVIS: And if they threw you away again tomorrow? Then would you choose us? Or should I extinguish this flame?

BAYARD:
Put out the light; and then, put out the light.
When I have pluck'd thy rose, I cannot give it
vital growth again, It must needs wither:—
O, balmy breath, that dost almost persuade
Justice to break her sword!
(He kisses DAVIS *three times, gently.)*
One more, one more;
One more, and this the last;
So sweet, I must weep.

(The violin and viola create beautiful harmony, but are not built to match tones or carry the same melody.)

DAVIS: Would now be a bad time to tell you I hate *Othello*? Communicating in code for two years and you couldn't choose a comedy?

BAYARD: It was the only one I knew by heart.

DAVIS: The Moor and fair Desdemona seems a little cliche and the casting predictable.

BAYARD: You are too marvelous for words. And you were always *just enough* for me. Compassionate, thoughtful, so sweet. But...Dear Heart, they would take you. And I'm not strong enough to see you hanging from a tree.

DAVIS: They're going to throw you away again.

BAYARD: Who?

(Intercom buzzes.)

(Enter MR RANDOLPH.*)*

MR RANDOLPH: Good Lord, Davis! Hello, son.

DAVIS: Hello, Mr Randolph.

MR RANDOLPH: Are you staying awhile?

DAVIS: No, sir. Heading to Penn Station now.

MR RANDOLPH: Are you alright, Bayard?

MOVEMENT TWO—ANTISTROPHE

DAVIS: He doesn't know, sir.

MR RANDOLPH: No one else has contacted you?

BAYARD: The power was down. What??

(MR RANDOLPH *turns on the radio.*)

MR RANDOLPH: Son, it has happened. I want you to brace yourself and say this prayer...

BAYARD: No prayers, Mr Randolph, what?!

RADIO: ...in preparation for the March on the Mall in three weeks. Heavy opposition from the President's administration has met the March organizers, and the fate of the once likely demonstration now seems to be in jeopardy.

BAYARD: Once likely?

RADIO: Senator Strom Thurmond took to the floor of Congress late this afternoon to submit criminal records of chief organizer, Bayard Rustin.

RADIO: *(Strom Thurmond. VO)* An immoral element is at the heart of this movement. Bayard Rustin. A draft-dodger, a member of the Communist party and known sexual pervert was arrested in Pasadena, California in 1953 on a morals charge. The term morals charge is true but this is a clear cut case of lessening the charge. The conviction was Sex Perversion.

(The RADIO *continues the news.)*

RADIO: More details are expected tomorrow as Negro Leaders are meeting this evening in New York City. J Edgar Hoover's office was not available for comment, although...

(MR RANDOLPH *turns off radio.*)

(The grandfather clock gongs, six times.)

MR RANDOLPH: Son!

(Silence)

BAYARD: *(Yelling off)* MIRIAM!?

(Re-enter MIRIAM *with a glass of water.)*

MIRIAM: Oh, Bayard! I'm so sorry.

BAYARD: All the provisions have been made. The signs are complete and you know how to make new ones if Mr Randolph changes his focus. The wall of port-a-potties is due for delivery at what time on the 28th?

MIRIAM: Four AM!

BAYARD: You'll coordinate with each community organizer and confirm participation and scheduling of bus drop off and pick up.

MIRIAM: Yes, Bayard.

BAYARD: Are the books balanced?

MR RANDOLPH: Bayard.

BAYARD: Are the books balanced, Miriam?

MIRIAM: We're even except for five hundred dollars. Not sure where.

BAYARD: Go retrieve the file marked RANDOLPH.

(MIRIAM *leaves the glass of water and exits.)*

MR RANDOLPH: Where are you going?

BAYARD: Running to catch a train.

MR RANDOLPH: Why?

BAYARD: WHY?? Did you hear that bastard call me out of my name in front of the whole country?

MR RANDOLPH: I heard a desperate man try to stop our movement.

BAYARD: I heard humiliation! And I'm not going to wait to be *excused* again. I've taken the maps and tasks out of my head and plastered them on the walls because I knew this was going to happen. I've been

MOVEMENT TWO—ANTISTROPHE 45

waiting for this. Miriam is trained, you are trained, the Leaders are trained, just add water and stir.

(MIRIAM *returns with the file and removes an envelope.*)

BAYARD: Miriam. After the March, a team of sanitation workers will be milling about to clean up the aftermath. Walk up to each one and hand them one of these crisp, ironed ten dollar bills. Say, "With gratitude for your service. From A Philip Randolph".

MIRIAM: Yes Bayard. (*She exits.*)

MR RANDOLPH: Have I ever denied you? Have I ever let you sink to the bottom of the ocean? So sure you've figured me out! So close and you throw it away? I've never been more disappointed with you in my life!

BAYARD: WHAT ELSE WILL HE HAVE ME DO?! I've given up everything! I worked! Resisted! Fasted! Gave up love! What else will He have me do??

MR RANDOLPH: SETTLE SON!!

BAYARD: (*To the heavens*) If my life is so disposable You can keep throwing me away, then finish me! (*To* MR RANDOLPH*)* I've been waiting and waiting and waiting for what?

MR RANDOLPH: Your time.

BAYARD: I'm out of time. Now I start running, again.

MR RANDOLPH: Turn back, Brave Heart.

BAYARD: In front of the whole country.

MR RANDOLPH: It's done! You knew it was coming and the shadows have come to light and, now, it's done!

BAYARD: It's a witch hunt!

MR RANDOLPH: You are entering the realm of executive leadership. A new dimension. This is your rite of passage: surviving a violent storm in the soul.

DAVIS: What assurance can you give Leadership won't toss him away again?

MR RANDOLPH: MIRIAM!

(Re-enter MIRIAM.)

MR RANDOLPH: The Leaders and I have met. Take this memorandum.

(MIRIAM notates.)

MR RANDOLPH: We, the black leaders of the Civil Rights movement and the leaders of the trade union movement and the leaders of the Jewish, Protestant, and Catholic church which are organizing this march, have absolute confidence in Bayard Rustin's ability, his integrity, and his commitment to nonviolence as the best way to bring about social change. He will continue to organize the March with our full and undivided support.

BAYARD: The senator is interested in me because he wants to destroy our movement. He won't get away with this.

(DAVIS exits. MIRIAM follows.)

BAYARD: I'm sorry, Mr Randolph.

MR RANDOLPH: Don't apologize. Say thank you.

BAYARD: Thank You?

MR RANDOLPH: I thought you were a believer? Look up and say, THANK YOU.

BAYARD: THANK YOU.

MR RANDOLPH: Now, let it heal.

BAYARD: Something is missing. MIRIAM.

(MIRIAM reenters.)

BAYARD: Note: "Church Mothers, Aunties and like-minded women: please wear pearls and gloves to the

March. Easter and/or Sunday going-to-meeting clothes are encouraged". If a *gay* man is going to throw this party, then the attire must be written on the invitation. Isn't that right, Davis? *(He notices* DAVIS *has left.)*

*(*MIRIAM *exits.)*

MR RANDOLPH: Your purpose is here, son. You understand? Call Ossie Davis. Get us more stars. We need all the support we can get. And, he'll do your introduction. I believe you've earned a place at the podium.

MIRIAM: *(OS)* Line 1, Bayard.

MR RANDOLPH: Stand tall, son. Our people have weathered greater storms than this and so shall you. *(He exits.)*

BAYARD: *(On phone)* Headquarters, Bayard speaking. Oh, I will be just fine, Sweet Mahalia. No, no, I was thinking: if I promise not to mouth the words right next to you, would you consider opening for Dr King with *I've Been Buked, and I've Been Scorned*? Sing a little for me please? And, take your time, Mahalia.

*(*BAYARD *is slowly bathed in the golden God light.)*

MIRIAM: *(OS or VO)*
I've been buked, Lord, and I've been scorned
I've been buked, Lord, and I've been scorned
I've been talked about, sho' as you was born

*(*BAYARD *drinks the glass of water.)*

BAYARD: *(To the heavens)* Thank you…thank you…thank you.

(Lights fade.)

END OF MOVEMENT TWO—ANTISTROPHE

MOVEMENT THREE—
EPODE,
OR, SUMMARY IN A DIFFERENT METRE

Section One

(Lights up on the Mall on Washington, DC, Reflecting Pool. Eve of The March. 8 PM)

(Enter MIRIAM. *She carries a clipboard and a large coffee. As she walks along the pool's edge towards center, the sound system becomes more distant.)*

(After listening to the sound check for a minute, she waves frantically across the pool. Yelling:)

MIRIAM: No! *(Sotto voce)* This isn't happening. Wait! Breathe, Miriam. *(Yelling)* YES! Try it again, please. I can't hear anything back here. These speakers are... *(She waves stop.)* I have very specific instructions, Mister Sound Sir. We specifically paid for the twenty thousand dollar package of equipment to avoid the back half of the mall from NOT hearing. *(Sotto voce)* Miriam? Huh. Can you fix this? No. For real? Yeah. Okay. *(Yelling)* BAYARD!! BAYARD!!

BAYARD: What is it?

MIRIAM: Brace yourself.

BAYARD: I've been braced since 1937, what is it?

MIRIAM: There's a problem with the sound equipment.

BAYARD: No problem. The Lincoln Memorial is there, the Washington Monument is here. I want sound for this quarter mile.

MIRIAM: Someone, it appears, has cut the wires to the speakers.

BAYARD: Which set of speakers?

MIRIAM: All of them.

BAYARD: All of them?

MIRIAM: *(Yelling)* ALL OF THEM, SOUND SIR?? *(To BAYARD)* Yes, ALL of them!

BAYARD: *(Yelling)* I personally checked all equipment and wiring prior to set up. How did this occur? Was it professionally done or can it be salvaged? *(Sotto voce)* I knew this would happen. Miriam, troubleshoot.

MIRIAM: Ummm...perhaps...the sound will travel if everyone is super duper quiet.

BAYARD: If we're lucky enough to have this mall packed, the only way to have order is if everyone can hear perfectly, without straining.

MIRIAM: Ummm... Maybe...the Leaders will have superpowers and can speak really, really loud. Maybe your guys' God will make you talk real super duper loud! You want some coffee? It's good!

BAYARD: Try to think clearly and come up with two solutions in the next four minutes.

MIRIAM: Of course you give a pop quiz the night before the test.

BAYARD: My staff always welcomes Calamity! Think quicker, dear. Three minutes and fifty-four seconds left. *(He starts off.)*

MIRIAM: Where are you going?

BAYARD: To make a call. Meanwhile, go stop that man.

MOVEMENT THREE—EPODE

MIRIAM: *(Yelling)* EXCUSE ME, SIR…STOP!!!

(MIRIAM *exits.* BAYARD *steps forward into a light; or, the phone.)*

BAYARD: Good evening, Ethel. Bayard Rustin for Bobby, please. Thank you. *(A beat)* Good evening, Mr Kennedy, forgive me for interrupting your family time but we have a dilemma that cannot wait. It appears that the wires to ALL of our speakers have been cut. There is a high probability that mass chaos could ensue if the crowd can't hear the guests. *(A beat)* I promised a full attempt at one hundred percent non-violence, but this proves to be a stain on my blueprint. I'll hold. Yes, thank you.

(MIRIAM *reenters steam-rolling.)*

MIRIAM: I got it! Option 1: A chain of bullhorns will pass the information from the steps of Lincoln to Zone 2 who will pass it via bullhorn to Zone 3 to 4 to 5 to…; Option 2: We cancel and reschedule for next Wednesday, same time, same place! Who are you talking to?

BAYARD: The Man about the speakers.

MIRIAM: Let me handle that! *(On phone)* Good evening. This is Miriam Caldwell. I arranged these speakers more than forty days ago and checked WEEKLY with your staff to ENSURE ALL WENT SMOOTHLY from pick up to installation to striking down of equipment! WHEN did your company decide to DOWNGRADE its attention to detail? Before or AFTER payment? MIRIAM CALDWELL! Where are you from, you talk funny—

(BAYARD *"snatches the phone".)*

BAYARD: *(Sotto voce)* He's a Kennedy. Hello? *(On phone)* Yes, Bobby. I'll keep holding.

MIRIAM: *(Sotto voce)* You said you were talking to "a man about the speakers".

BAYARD: I said, "*The* Man about the speakers". You know, like, THE WHITE MAN!

MIRIAM: Do Freedom Fighters take naps??

BAYARD: *(On phone)* Yes, Bobby!? No, that was my assistant. Very good, I'll expect them. Please do. And thank you.

MIRIAM: Breathe, Miriam. This is all just a nightmare. A nightmare pop quiz or an open book test you are getting an "F" on. What can Bobby Kennedy do at eight at night that we couldn't??

(On cue, a loud helicopter hovers overhead.)

BAYARD: The Army Signal Corp. Welcome, gentlemen! You have twelve hours. GO!!

MIRIAM: Can I do anything else?

BAYARD: One. Stop being so hard on yourself. Two. Send a thank you note to Burke Marshall at the Justice Department tomorrow. Say—

MIRIAM: 'On behalf of A. Philip Randolph, for your emergency support'.

BAYARD: Three. Take a cat nap in the station wagon. *(A beat)* You're losing nap time, RUN RUN FAST FAST. *(A beat)* What is it?

MIRIAM: I've tried to hold my tongue, but I can't sit still and watch a team of civil rights leaders fail this test.

BAYARD: Which test?

MIRIAM: You failed to invite a single female speaker to the podium.

(BAYARD is caught off guard.)

BAYARD: Troubleshoot.

MOVEMENT THREE—EPODE

(Without missing a beat:)

MIRIAM: Contact Mrs Medgar Evers and Ms Diane Nash. Arrange five to six notables for a Tribute to… Negro Women Fighters for Freedom. Daisy Bates should speak before John Lewis.

BAYARD: You like Daisy Bates?

MIRIAM: Ouuu, yes! I make all my own clothes and because she looks like she floated off the cover of Ebony magazine while fighting Racism and Hatred, I tend to favor her style.

BAYARD: Then by all means, proceed. Good thinking, Ms. Caldwell.

MIRIAM: Thank you, Mr Rustin. What about Leadership?

BAYARD: I'll handle the Leaders. You handle him.

(MIRIAM spots a violator and charges after him.)

MIRIAM: EXCUSE ME, SIR! DO YOU HAVE A PERMIT FOR THAT??

(Phone rings. BAYARD answers.)

BAYARD: Washington Headquarters.

(MR RANDOLPH appears in a light.)

MR RANDOLPH: Bayard. Mr Randolph.

BAYARD: Yes sir.

MR RANDOLPH: Trouble.

BAYARD: Always.

MR RANDOLPH: The gentlemen are unsettled about the speaking arrangements. What shall I tell them?

BAYARD: Adhere to the line up I provide.

MR RANDOLPH: They're jockeying for better press positioning. You have Martin buried at the end of the program.

BAYARD: Vaudeville, Phil. The best act is always second to last. Plus, not a single reporter will leave until AFTER the newborn King's words of wisdom. Trust me.

MR RANDOLPH: I do. I'll report. John Lewis is upset that we have not approved his speech?

BAYARD: Tell him we haven't because he hasn't made the necessary changes. Phrases like "taking by force" and "marching like Sherman did" are not...

MR RANDOLPH: ...I understand, but what do I tell him?

BAYARD: "SETTLE, SON!" This is not about him, this is not about me, this is about a day for our great grandparents and their mothers and fathers. We hear him, I even agree, but tell him to adjust or be adjusted out. WAIT. Voting Rights Act, next. We promise.

MR RANDOLPH: I agree. We'll speak shortly.

(MR RANDOLPH *exits. Phones ring.* BAYARD *answers.*)

BAYARD: Washington Headquarters.

(MARTIN *appears in a light.*)

MARTIN: Bayard. Martin.

BAYARD: King.

MARTIN: I'm not sure about this, Bayard. I'm not...

BAYARD: Stop. You are fine. You are ready.

MARTIN: My staff is urging me NOT to talk about my dream. They feel it's too soft for the day.

BAYARD: Fire them! Fire them, all. *(A beat)* Martin?

MARTIN: I'm nervous about all of this attention.

BAYARD: Good. I'd be worried if you weren't. All you Baptists get nervous before public speaking.

MARTIN: The Nation of Islam is calling this the Farce on Washington.

MOVEMENT THREE—EPODE

BAYARD: Tomorrow I want you to stand at the base of Lincoln's feet, stare out a mile ahead of you and speak on behalf of the slaves. Preach your dream. Paint it as you see it. Testify to all those who will call us Uncle Toms for doing God's will, and if it isn't in His will for them to join us, let them go. Or, as we New Yorkers say, fuck 'em!

(MARTIN laughs.)

BAYARD: I won't let them touch you, Martin. You have my word.

MARTIN: I hear you won't be joining us at the White House after the March?

(A beat)

BAYARD: My invitation must've gotten lost in the mail. We'll talk soon. You stay focused.

(MARTIN exits. Phone rings. BAYARD answers.)

BAYARD: Washington Headquarters. Bobby, they arrived right on cue. Mr Kennedy, when God wants us to hear Him, He comes in a still, quiet spirit or, yes, a loud test. Which do you think this is?

(The speakers echo: "TESTING TESTING".)

BAYARD: You heard that, yes? Mr Kennedy, I'm thinking of running for President in '64 and am considering you for my running mate. A Quaker and a Catholic walk into a bar...

(Dial tone. BAYARD smiles, slyly.)

(He steps forward into a golden God light.)

BAYARD: Ma! I can feel you. I feel you whispering, "Make a memory. Don't forget to remember to remember this." I will remember loving this organized chaos. I will remember this heat, hotter than the hate in the belly of ole Bull Conner, and yet, the gentlest, kindest breeze. I remember every Christmas Uncle

James would telephone and recite *Lift Ev'ry Voice and Sing*, just to me. Ma, call forth James Weldon Johnson and ask if I may stand on his words, today. And, if you are passing by the Lord, see if today pleases Him? Tell Him I'm painting this portrait to look like the elegance of Easter, but it feels like...

(The sounds of the crowd gathering for a great symphony.)

BAYARD: I will remember this feels just like the childlike giddiness of Christmas Eve!

(End of Section One)

Section Two

(The March montage)

(Suggested staging. Director's interpretive choice)

(A musicalized version of Lift Ev'ry Voice and Sing—*a commemorative poem circa 1900, celebrating the birth of Abraham Lincoln—commences. Perhaps Merry Clayton's soul-shouting rendition.)*

*(*BAYARD *conducts a digital media symphony of projected photos and moving images from the day. He is in total control of every aspect of this music video which utilizes technology to represent his genius mind 50+ years ahead of its time.)*

*(*MR RANDOLPH *announces speakers as* MIRIAM *assists* BAYARD. *She then conducts the second verse dedicated to the female presence on the day. Images of: Lena Horne, Josephine Baker, Myrlie Evers...etc.)*

(At "Sing, sing it out, sing..." MARTIN *appears and delivers the following text [author's paraphrasing] to replicate "I Have a Dream":)*

("I proclaim today standing in the majestic gaze of Lincoln, that someday, maybe not today, but one day,

MOVEMENT THREE—EPODE

the Divine Visions of Heaven will trickle down like gentle raindrops on Oppression. Then, every American can shout: Free at last, free at last, I thank God Who is Mighty, I'm Free At Last.")

(The crowd goes wild.)

(Regret cleared, MR RANDOLPH exits. MIRIAM follows.)

(BAYARD conducts the final refrain with Divine Stamina. Headlines read: "Over 250,000 Pour In"; President Welcomes Negro Leadership at White House"; "No Incidents Reported"; "America's Finest Day".)

(The final image projected: Dr Martin Luther King's outstretched hand waving over a sea of people.)

(Bayard buttons the song and exits.)

(Applause)

(Projections/BAYARD VO of the Demands from the March On Washington pamphlet:)

BAYARD: *(VO)* We demand that segregation be ended in every school district in the year 1963.

We demand that we have comprehensive and effective civil rights legislation from the present Congress—without compromise or filibuster—to guarantee all Americans access to all public accommodations; decent housing; adequate and integrated education and the right to vote.

(Read as many Demands necessary to cover the transition from Washington back to Harlem.)

BAYARD: *(VO)* What say you!?

(Massive applause)

(Projection in Technicolor: Bayard Rustin and A Philip Randolph on the cover of LIFE magazine.)

(End of March montage.)

CODA; OR, PASSAGE BRINGING A MOVEMENT TO A CLOSE

(Lights up. Three weeks later. Headquarters and Ebenezer Baptist Church.)

(Enter MR RANDOLPH *with a letter-sized gift box.)*

MR RANDOLPH: Nowhere!

BAYARD: Really?! Nowhere!

MR RANDOLPH: Not anywhere!

BAYARD: Did you check on...

MR RANDOLPH: 145th—

BAYARD: 128th—

MR RANDOLPH: The newsstand by the subway entrance—

BAYARD: Nowhere, really?

MR RANDOLPH: Nowhere. I cannot secure a copy of *LIFE* magazine anywhere.

BAYARD: That is tremendous. You are officially a star.

(Enter MIRIAM.*)*

MIRIAM: Bayard. Everything is spotless and my bus leaves in an hour...oh, forgive me. Hello, sir.

MR RANDOLPH: Hello, Dear. Bayard has you in on a Sunday?

MIRIAM: Reverend King agreed to have this morning's sermon broadcast for the Associated Press. It's almost show time.

MR RANDOLPH: I see an extra bounce in your step.

BAYARD: It's her last day.

MIRIAM: Everyday since The March I've beat the sun waking up. Been walking tall with newfound hope. What a wonderful gift.

MR RANDOLPH: Where to next?

MIRIAM: Heading home to start a new position for the NAACP—*Advisor for the Women's Legal Fund.* Thanks to you both, and Daisy Bates for this outfit, I am ready to use these blueprints for Women. Thank you, Mr Randolph, for your kindness.

(MIRIAM *offers a firm handshake.* MR RANDOLPH *proudly shakes back.*)

BAYARD: Upstairs has been cleaned out so now we can shift this platform for protest into a Coalition for social change! Bring these bickering brilliant minds together. May I begin staffing up?

MR RANDOLPH: I have spoken with Leadership. We feel it best to dismantle this office.

BAYARD: Why?

MR RANDOLPH: For the same reason we dismantled the March in '41—we achieved our objectives. However, there is still great work to be done. I used to regret that Lucille and I are childless, but I've been sent a son to carry out my visions. For your services. *(He extends the gift box.)*

BAYARD: Cranes Stationery. Should I thank you or Lucille?

MR RANDOLPH: Make sure it's the weight you prefer. You write so damn hard.

CODA

(BAYARD *opens the stationery.*)

BAYARD: *A Philip Randolph Institute. Bayard Rustin, Executive Director.*

MR RANDOLPH: It'll take a year or two to set up but I have a few more portraits I'd like to commission.

BAYARD: ...Thank you.

(*The phone rings.* BAYARD *answers.*)

BAYARD: A Philip Randolph Institute, Bayard Rustin, Executive Director speaking.

MR RANDOLPH: It's not official yet, son!

(*Lights up on* MARTIN. *Sounds of chaos behind.*)

MARTIN: Bayard. Martin. I TOLD YOU. I said it. I said it plain.

BAYARD: Reverend King, we agreed. Two microphones, no cameras...

MARTIN: I TOLD you. I said it. I TOLD you it wasn't over.

BAYARD: Wait, wait, wait. What are you going on about?

MARTIN: Turn on the news!

(BAYARD *turns on the radio.*)

RADIO (*VO*) ...The explosion hit the Sixteenth Street Baptist Church as morning worship services were beginning. An apparent bombing by the local Birmingham chapter of the Ku Klux Klan comes just three weeks after the March on Washington brought the races together. Officials say the death toll, at the moment, is estimated at four girls who were trapped in the basement when the explosion hit..."

MIRIAM: No!

MR RANDOLPH: My my my.

MARTIN: In Sunday School. They're blowing up our churches.

MR RANDOLPH: Coretta?

BAYARD: Are Coretta and the children accounted for?

MARTIN: They're all fine, but I can't preach.

BAYARD: You have to. No fear.

Miriam begins to hyperventilate.

MARTIN: I feel like imploding! Damn! Maybe we were wrong, maybe we...

BAYARD: Martin. Stop. Breathe. This is it. Everything we have ever discussed from the very beginning of the beginning counts NOW. The March was your dress rehearsal.

MARTIN: My mouth tastes revenge. I'm seeing red.

MIRIAM: I can't...I can't breathe...

(MR RANDOLPH *attends to* MIRIAM.)

BAYARD: There is a live feed in your sanctuary, Martin. The ear of the nation is resting in your pulpit. Remember your audience. Remember the folk who don't know nor care to know Jesus but need your instructions, too.

MARTIN: I need to take care of *my* congregation this morning.

BAYARD: You belong to the world, now. Reassure your flock, and the rest. That's your task.

(MARTIN *hangs up.* BAYARD *races to* MIRIAM.)

MR RANDOLPH: Son...

MIRIAM: I—I wait. I don't understand how—

BAYARD: Breathe, breathe.

MIRIAM: Wait wait!

CODA

(The phone rings. MR RANDOLPH *answers.)*

MR RANDOLPH: Martin? Hello, Mr President, Mr Randolph. We just did. Yes sir, a symbolic gesture on the Mall would be most appropriate. Yes, right away. Be safe, Mr President. *(He hangs up.)* I'm on a flight to DC.

BAYARD: Should I come with?

MR RANDOLPH: Close out the office. The Great Ms Miriam Caldwell. I expect to hear great things from you.

MIRIAM: We'll likely be doing them together, sir. If you'll have me.

MR RANDOLPH: It would be an honor. *(He collects his hat. To* BAYARD:*)* Now you are the leader you so fervently wished to be. A lesson. After every victory, there will be a storm. The picnic is over, son. *(He exits.)*

BAYARD: What do we do first, Miriam?

MIRIAM: I'm sorry?

BAYARD: Think. Quick. Tragedy. What do we do first?

MIRIAM: Grieve.

BAYARD: The parents own custody of that emotion. What are YOU going to do?

MIRIAM: Call them.

BAYARD: You don't know them.

MIRIAM: Send flowers.

BAYARD: Out of what budget? Where to? Is this the time for flowers?

MIRIAM: I don't know.

BAYARD: Well while you figure the answer I need to… pray. Care to join me?

MIRIAM: I told you I don't believe in fairy tales.

BAYARD: Fine. Excuse me for a moment.

(MIRIAM *attempts to hug* BAYARD.)

BAYARD: Run to your bus, dear. I'm about to break.

(MIRIAM *exits.*)

(BAYARD *slams the stationery on the desk, violently.*)

BAYARD: *(To the heavens)*
Oh, foul, foul God! What bitter fruit is this?
Not manna that rained down for Israelites;
But strange and bitter fruit for dark hued tribes.
Wonder, I will not. Ask, I shall not.
Beg. Yes, I will. I beg you, *please* Father. Take me. Not the babies.

(*The* RADIO *turns on, by itself, in a golden glow.* BAYARD *is taken aback.*)

(KING/RADIO *in tandem with* BAYARD's *prayer.*)

KING/RADIO: Moses said, *Please let me see your glory!*

BAYARD: I lay down my life before the enemy and say, Take me!

KING/RADIO: The Lord said, *I will let all my goodness pass in front of you.*

BAYARD: I'm not afraid of resting with Jesus, but those girls were just meeting Him.

KING/RADIO: —*and there*—

BAYARD: In Sunday school, Father??

KING/RADIO: —*there I will call out my name, the Lord. I will be kind to anyone I want to.*

BAYARD: Reconsider.

KING/RADIO: *I will be merciful to anyone I want to.*

BAYARD: SHOW YOUR FACE, COWARD!

KING/RADIO: —*but you cannot see my face, because no one may see me and live.*

CODA

BAYARD: Do you not see me? Do you not see us? They're assassinating our children.

KING/RADIO: This morning, let us be mindful of the necessity of faith.

BAYARD: I've run this race to show you my faith.

KING/RADIO: However, faith without works is dead.

BAYARD: I've not rested until I proven to you my faith.

KING/RADIO: I say to you, standing in the center of the most dangerous place to be this Sunday morning.

BAYARD: I forfeit my faith! I forfeit my faith!

Bayard goes to the hidden door.

KING/RADIO: Now is not the time to wait for a miracle. Now is the hour to reach down, deep beneath the bottom of your bellies and grip tight the Divine remedy sent down through the ages—

BAYARD: *(To* ANCESTORS*)* How did you all learn—

KING/RADIO: —*forgiveness.*

BAYARD: —*forgiveness.*

KING/RADIO: Non violence is a practice, a daily discipline to help sustain our spirits on the long, tedious journey, ahead. It takes a lot of courage to be still.

(BAYARD *falls to his knees.)*

BAYARD: If your will has been done Father, then I concede, I relinquish the reins.

KING/RADIO: Surrender.

BAYARD: Just tell me those young ladies made it home.

KING/RADIO: Let your bodies be used on the front lines of Justice! Know that your light shines special and isn't made to look like anyone else's. Let your purpose be made evident through your works, your actions, all our deeds. Not just our words.

(BAYARD, *childlike, sings the Quaker tune* Walk in the Light.)

BAYARD: *There's a Light that was shining when the world began—*

KING/RADIO: I'm reminded of a song we teach our children in Sunday school.

BAYARD: *And a Light that is shining in the heart of man.*

KING/RADIO: Every culture has its own traditions.

BAYARD:
There's a Light that is shining in the Turk and the Jew
And a Light that is shining, friend, in me and you.

BAYARD: *(Throws his hands up)* I surrender.

(*The Baptist spiritual* Walk in the Light *plays on the piano, magically.*)

KING/RADIO: One of the first songs we teach them, based on John 1:7 says, *But if we walk in the light, as He, Himself, is also in the light, we have fellowship with one another…*

(*A beautiful, vivid, white light slowly grows inside the office, embracing* BAYARD.)

KING/RADIO: While the enemy has spilt the blood of our daughters, a permanent reminder of how well the evil-doers can do; I smile knowing four vibrant spirits were met by an arrrmy of loving angels, this morning!

(REVEREND KING'S CHOIR *[radio] and the* ANCESTORS—*fully alive inside the white light—sing, triumphantly.*)

REVEREND KING'S CHOIR/ANCESTORS:
Walk in the light, Beautiful light
Sung where the dew drops of mercy shine bright

CODA

Shine all around us, by day and by night
Jesus, the light of the world.

(BAYARD *stands in the center of the white light. Overcome, he sees his mother.*)

BAYARD: *(To the light)* MA! Ma. Show me those girls, Ma!

KING/RADIO: Today, the nation remembers: Addie Mae Collins; Cynthia Wesley; Carole Robertson; Denise McNair.

(Projections: portraits of Addie Mae Collins; Cynthia Wesley; Carole Robertson; Denise McNair.)

(BAYARD *sees four vibrants colors inside the white light.*)

KING/RADIO: Let us be silent.

BAYARD: *(To the Heavens)* Lord, settle my spirit and prepare my mind, for, NOW, Lord, I am ready to be used. However You so choose. Give me strength to brave the storms ahead and the courage to stand in the center of exactly who You called me to be. For You will be with me Always.

(The white light transitions back to a golden God light—God's constant presence—illuminating BAYARD, *the piano, and the radio.)*

KING/RADIO: It's not over. God spoke it to me.

BAYARD: I heard Him.

(The piano concludes with a simple "Amen" ending.)
(God light fades.)

END OF ODE

www.ingramcontent.com/pod-product-compliance
Lightning Source LLC
Chambersburg PA
CBHW060216050426
42446CB00013B/3091